D0622857

WE WERE HERE FIRST
THE NATIVE AMERICANS

THE
SEMINOLE

Wayne L. Wilson

PURPLE TOAD
PUBLISHING

WE WERE HERE FIRST
THE NATIVE AMERICANS

Publisher's Cataloging-in-Publication Data
Wilson, Wayne L.
    Seminole / written by Wayne L. Wilson.
        p. cm.
Includes bibliographic references, glossary, and
index.
    ISBN 9781624693120
1. Seminole Indians--Juvenile literature. 2. Indians
of North America--Southern States--Juvenile
literature. I. Series: We Were Here First: The Native
Americans.
  E99.S28 2017
  975.90049
Library of Congress Control Number: 2016957223

eBook ISBN: 9781624693137

CONTENTS

In 1840, artist George Catlin painted a portrait of a Seminole boy named Osceola (Asi-Yahola) Nick-a-no-chee, who was about nine years old. When Seminole boys turn twelve, they take part in a "black drink" ceremony, in which they leave childhood behind.

CHAPTER 1
THE
CEREMONY

Billy Powell excitedly helped clear the forest of grass, brush, and wildflowers. He and a few other teenage boys were clearing a dance site for a ceremony later that day. Billy was an apprentice to Abiaka, the most powerful medicine man in the land. Abiaka taught him the powers of plants. He made medicines to protect warriors in battle.[1]

Billy hustled with the other boys. They piled most of the plants away from the clearing, but they also gathered herbs. Abiaka would use these for his medicines. They also gathered the leaves of holly bushes, which Abiaka would brew to make a ceremonial "black drink." When a boy drank the black drink, it was a symbol that youth was gone and the boy had become a man.

The Green Corn Ceremony was the most important ritual for the Seminoles. The festival celebrated the corn harvest. It also thanked the Creator for providing the tribe with food and life. When the corn was ripe, the four-day ceremony began. No one was allowed to eat any corn until all the religious rites were completed.

The Green Corn Ceremony is held during the summer. It is marked by singing, dancing, feasting, and fasting.

The Green Corn Ceremony was celebrated as a New Year, as a time for renewing life. Old fires were put out, villages were cleaned, women designed new clothes, and worn pottery was broken and replaced.[2] Feuds and arguments were settled and forgotten. Men and women separated into different camps according to their clan.

In the center of the dance circle, men laid four logs in the shape of a cross. The chief built a new fire with the logs. Then he lighted sticks to give to each house so that families could start the year with a new fire.

The crackling flames leaped from the grandfather fire. They lit up Billy's face as he gazed into what he saw as a sacred living being. The Seminole were taught that the prayers of the people are passed to the Master of Breath through fire.[3]

The ceremony included prayers, fasting, joyous celebrations, and serious talks about life. The dancing symbolized the tribe's social and spiritual life. People danced for hours under the stars, performing a stomp-and-shuffle style of the dance. Non-natives call it the "stomp dance." In the Muscogee language, the dance is called *opvnkv hacogee*, meaning "drunken," "crazy," or "spirited."[4]

As the medicine man chanted, Billy and other male dancers followed behind him single file, loudly answering his verses. The women danced in silence, except for the noise made from shakers tied to their legs.

On the dawn of the final day of ceremony, the women left to prepare a feast of meat and corn. The men and boys took part in a bloodletting ceremony. Thorns or other sharp objects were used in a ritual to tear open the flesh. They believed that carving deep gashes on the arms, legs, or chest would purify the blood, prevent illness, and ensure a long life.[5]

Three Seminole medicine men with Chief Corey Osceola (on the right) in the 1920s. Medicine men not only treated aches, pains, and illness, but provided help with personal problems.

Chief Satouriona Prepares His Men for Battle, **an engraving made in 1564 by Jacques Le Moyne. The engraving shows the importance of ceremony before battle.**

Next, Billy drank the "black drink." The harsh tea made him vomit, but it purged the bad spirits and sickness from his body. It would make him invincible in war. As he drank he impressed the men by singing. Like a snake's skin, he shed his childhood name forever. He was renamed Asi-Yahola, "Black Drink Singer."

In English, he would be known as Osceola. He would become a famous warrior and leader of the Seminole Tribe of Florida.

Seminole Words

English	Seminole
Bed	*topa*
Bird	*fuswa*
Boy	*che-paw-nee*
Ceremony	*mistehoka*
Deer	*echo*
Eat	*hom-pus-che*
Father	*chacteka*
Fire	*totika*
Girl	*hok-to-che*
Heart	*efeki*
Hunger	*e-la-we*
Indian	*stechali*
Man	*han-nah-wah*
Money	*chatta kanah wah*
Mother	*chatske*
Night	*yomot-skay*
Owl	*huppe*
Peace	*esse-ka-putcha-la*
Rattlesnake	*chitta-micco*
Sun	*hasse*
Tree	*itto*
Victory cry	*caha-queene*
War	*so-lee-tah-wah*
Woman	*hokte*
Year	*yeske*

Leroy Osceola, a Miccosukee Seminole, is an artist and canoe maker. He leads a traditional life in a Miccosukee camp off the Tamiami Trail in Florida.

CHAPTER 2
THE
BEGINNINGS

"We were here first . . . then the other countries came," says Leroy Osceola, tribal councilman of the Sovereign Miccosukee Seminole Nation. "First the Vikings arrived and we fought them off, then the Spaniards came and we battled them, the English showed up and we fought them, too. In our wars with the United States, the army wiped out most of the people on the Indian reservations and took away their lands, but we're the only ones that never surrendered. We've never accepted the reservations and still live on our own lands. We are unconquered and undefeated."

At the end of several wars between the United States and the Seminoles, about 3,000 Seminoles were forced to move. The new Indian territory was west of the Mississippi River, mainly in Oklahoma. Over 300 Seminoles escaped capture by the U.S. army during the 1800s, fighting the troops in and around the Florida Everglades. After a while, the U.S. government ended the chase. Today, the descendants of these courageous Seminoles call themselves the "Unconquered People."

The Landing of Columbus, an oil painting by John
Vanderlyn, glamorizes Columbus as discovering America.
Native Americans view him as an invader, not a discoverer.

By the time Columbus made his voyage to the New World in 1492, there
were over 100,000 Florida Indians living throughout the territory. Tribes
such as the Timucuans lived in the northeast. The Apalachee and Pensacola
lived in the northwest. The Tocobaga were in the west-central Florida. The
Calusa lived in the southwest.[1] They had been there for thousands of years
before the Europeans arrived. In the early 1500s, the English, French, and

Spanish came to the New World. They fought for power and competed for the riches in this new territory.

By the 1800s, the Spaniards had nearly wiped out tribes such as the Tequestas, Calusas, Apalachees, and Timucuans. Spanish greed and war were direct causes. Indirect causes were diseases the Spaniards brought, such as smallpox. Scholars estimate that out of the 100,000 Native Americans living in Florida during the 1500s, fewer than 50 survived.[2]

The Seminole Nation began to form in the eighteenth century. Bands of Native Americans, mostly Muscogee, moved into northern Florida from Georgia, Mississippi, and Alabama. African Americans who fled from slavery in South Carolina and Georgia joined them. The British called the Muscogee the Creeks because their villages were close to creeks and rivers.[3] The word *Seminole* means "wild" or "runaway people."

Canoes were one of the main forms of transportation used by Native American tribes that lived near rivers, lakes, and oceans.

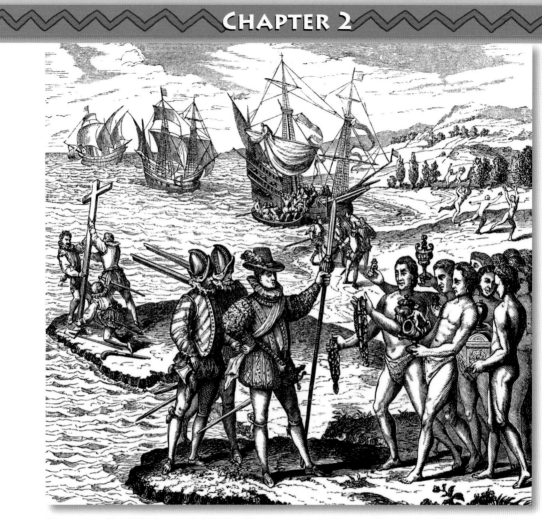

Between the 1400s and 1800s, European explorers brought diseases such as smallpox, influenza, measles, and the bubonic plague. These diseases ravaged the Native American population.

Many of the Lower Creeks moved from their town in the second half of the eighteenth century. To escape conflicts with the Upper Creeks and colonists, they moved into northern Florida. In 1767, Europeans moving south forced the Upper Creeks of Alabama to also move into Florida. They joined forces with the growing Seminole Nation.[4]

In 1778, other tribes joined the Seminoles. These included the Hitichis, and Yamasees of Georgia, the Apalachees of Florida, the Alabamas and Mobiles of Alabama, and also the Choctaws, Chickasaws, and Houmas of Mississippi.

Everett Osceola is Cultural Ambassador of the Seminole Tribe of Florida. He explains, "The Seminoles were a mixture of different tribes, from all different camps, and we banded together to survive and try to keep our way of life."

For Native Americans and fugitive slaves, Spanish Florida offered a safe haven from slavery. As Assistant Chief Lewis Johnson of the Oklahoma Seminole Nation explains, the Spanish Crown openly invited the Muscogee, Miccosukee, and Hitchiti groups to come and live there. Runaway slaves were given land, and entire communities of blacks lived freely under Spanish

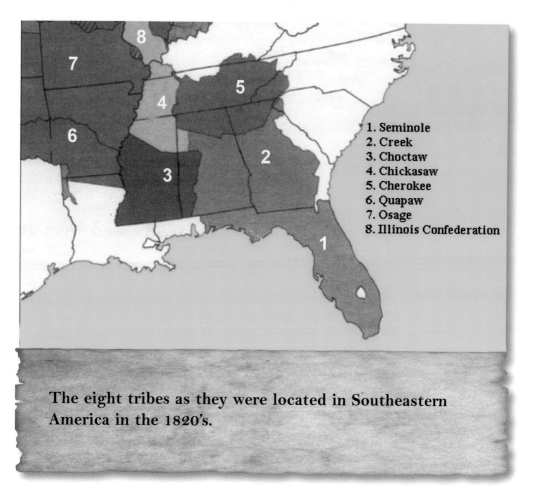

1. Seminole
2. Creek
3. Choctaw
4. Chickasaw
5. Cherokee
6. Quapaw
7. Osage
8. Illinois Confederation

The eight tribes as they were located in Southeastern America in the 1820's.

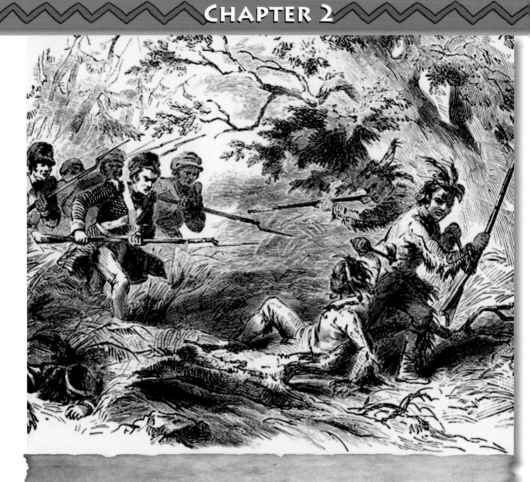

European settlers and the U.S. government forced the Creek from their homelands. Many tribes moved to Florida and joined the Seminole Nation.

rule in Florida. The Spanish often recruited African Americans to fight in their militia against the British.

Osceola and his mother were among the Alabama Creek who moved to Florida. He remembered the injustices he suffered as a child. He and his family ran after they were held captive. They had watched soldiers destroy and burn their ancestral home and murder innocent loved ones. He never forgot Abiaka's lectures that he must always resist efforts by the outsiders to remove them from their homelands. As an adult, he would not move again.

The Black Seminoles

Black Seminoles lived in villages near the Seminoles.
They formed their own groups called Freedman
bands. Today, Freedman bands are represented on the
General Council of the Seminole Nation.

The Black Seminoles were free blacks and runaway slaves called Maroons.
These fugitive slaves and freedman lived and worked with the Seminoles.
They also adopted many Seminole customs and clothing styles, and some of
them married Seminoles. They lived in their own villages close to the Indian
settlements, owned livestock, had their own chiefs, and practiced their
African religion and customs.[5]

The Black Seminoles were excellent farmers and builders. Because they
spoke English, they often acted as interpreters and traders for the Seminole.
As warriors, the Black Seminoles were highly respected for their skill and
bravery.

After the battle of Horseshoe Bend, Chief William "Red Eagle" Weatherford surrendered to General Andrew Jackson.

CHAPTER 3
INVADERS, WAR, AND RELOCATION

Once the Revolutionary War ended in 1783, the demand for slavery rose. Slavers were angry that the Seminoles were harboring their former slaves. They formed citizen militias from Alabama, Georgia, and Tennessee. Their plan was to march into north-central Florida and destroy the tribe's farms and villages.[1]

The Seminole discovered their plans and attacked their plantations first. In retaliation, Major General Andrew Jackson assembled troops and crossed into Florida. During 1813 and 1814, the soldiers destroyed many Creek towns in Florida.

The Upper Creek Indians abandoned the area and joined the Seminoles, tripling their population. Most were Muscogee speakers, and this helped the tribes to communicate.

The First Seminole War started at Fort Negro. Located on the Apalachicola River near Georgia, it was once a British fort. After the British left, it served as a refuge for hundreds of runaway slaves. The fort was heavily supplied with arms and ammunition.

Fearing a slave rebellion, Andrew Jackson, known as "Sharp Knife" by the Seminole, ordered American troops to attack the fort and return the slaves to their owners. The troops surrounded the fort, ordering the fugitive slaves to surrender. They refused. Shots were exchanged. At one point, a heated cannonball hit

Andrew Jackson, who became president of the United States, was a wealthy slave owner. He was known as "Indian killer" and "Sharp Knife" because of his brutal military action against Native Americans. He was the main force behind the devastating 1830 Indian Removal Act.

the fort's powder magazines. It caused an enormous explosion that leveled the fort and killed over 350 men, women, and children.

The Seminoles were furious about this brutal act. They attacked settlers living near the border between Florida and Georgia In 1817, American soldiers crossed the border to the Seminole village of Fowl Town. They killed people, looted the town, and burned it to the ground. The survivors fled into the swamplands.

As the First Seminole War continued, Jackson attacked towns along the Suwannee River in Georgia. He then marched his troops through East Florida, burning crops and destroying Seminole villages.[2]

Spain turned Florida over to the United States in 1819. Two years later, Jackson was appointed governor. Native Americans and escaped slaves who fled into Florida to be free found themselves once again living in U.S. territory.

At that time, the "Five Civilized Tribes"—Cherokee, Chickasaw, Choctaw, Muscogee Creek, and Seminole—lived on millions of acres of land in Mississippi, Georgia, Alabama, Tennessee, South Carolina, and Florida. These southeastern nations were called "civilized" because some adopted European clothing, farming tools, housing, and religion.[3]

U.S. government leaders plotted how they could gain this land for European settlers. President Thomas Jefferson wanted to force the Indians to give up their cultures, customs, religions, and lifestyles. Ultimately, he figured, they would also give up their land.

To avoid war, several chiefs and over 400 Seminoles met with government agents in 1823. They signed a treaty of "peace and friendship" at Moultrie Creek, Florida.[4] Under the terms of the treaty, the Seminoles gave up all claims to lands in Florida for reservation land of four million acres.

Only a few more than a thousand Seminoles moved to the reservation in central Florida. Many refused to leave the land of their birth. The reservation land was so terrible, even the best farmers would have had trouble raising crops there. Game was scarce. The treaty also allowed white slave owners to

According to the Treaty of Moultrie Creek, 1823, the U.S. government established a reservation for the Seminoles in the middle of Florida. Six chiefs were allowed to keep their villages along the Apalachicola River. However, the land was largely unsuitable for hunting or farming, and the majority of Seminoles refused to move to the reservation.

come onto the reservation and seize black members of the tribe. The Seminoles refused to let these members be taken. Slave owners and bounty hunters stormed into the governor's office, demanding he enforce the treaty.

On May 28, 1830, Congress passed the Indian Removal Act, setting the stage for one of the most shameful periods in American history. The government gave itself authority to remove all Five Civilized Tribes east of the Mississippi River to Indian Territory in Arkansas and Oklahoma.[5] Native Americans were forced to make the deadly trek on the "Trail of Tears" to the Southwest. Black freedmen and slaves living with the Indians joined them. The marchers faced starvation, disease, and murder. Many of the men were shackled for this march. Thousands of people died on the trail. Many of the Seminole were also removed by ship through the Gulf of Mexico. They landed in New Orleans before marching to the reservations.

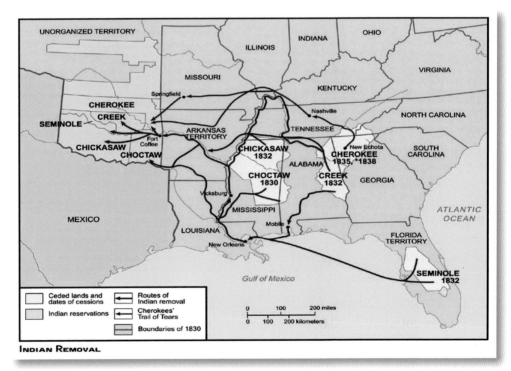

INDIAN REMOVAL

The five Southeastern tribes were forced to leave their homelands and live in Indian Territory.

Some Indians refused to leave. The U.S. government decided to remove them by force. The result was the Second Seminole War.

On December 28, 1835, U.S. troops met Seminole warriors led by Micanopy, Jumper, and Alligator.[6] In this battle, 108 soldiers lost their lives. Four days later, Osceola, with only 250 warriors, defeated 750 soldiers in the Battle of Withlacoochee. He vowed to fight for his land "until the last drop of Seminole blood moistened the dust of my hunting ground."[7]

Osceola (Asi-yahola) became one of the most influential leaders in Seminole history. Handsome, passionate, brave, an elegant dresser, and great speaker, Osceola developed brilliant combat strategies, often leaving U.S. generals surprised and confused.

Battles and skirmishes raged along the Florida Peninsula. Though out-gunned and outnumbered, the Seminoles fought brilliantly using guerrilla warfare. Osceola, Jumper, Alligator, and Micanopy, with fewer than 3,000 fighters, fought against 30,000 U.S. soldiers.[8]

Osceola and his warriors continued to foil U.S. forces. Desperate army leaders switched to trickery. Flying a flag of truce and offering to discuss peace, the U.S. military lured Osceola and his warriors into a trap. Osceola was captured and imprisoned. He died from illness in prison in 1838.[9]

Osceola was captured and arrested in 1837 on the orders of the deceitful General Thomas Jesup.

In 2016, Assistant Chief Johnson said this about Osceola's legacy:

> *Osceola was never an inherited mekko or chief, but he was a great tustenugge (warrior). He inspired the people. Osceola will always be a revered warrior . . . one who fought for sovereignty. Osceola was about living as our people lived—freely. That's what makes great warriors fighters for causes. They don't just believe it . . . they live it. And will die for it if they have to.[10]*

The United States believed Osceola's capture and death would end the war, but the battles continued until 1842. No peace treaty was ever signed. It is reported that 3,800 Seminoles were relocated to the Indian Territory,

The Seminoles used the trees in the swamp to hide from patrols.

mostly in Oklahoma. About 300 Seminoles remained free by hiding deep into the Florida Everglades.

In 1855, a Third Seminole War began when Chief Billy Bowlegs attacked a survey party in Collier County, Florida. The series of battles over land conflicts lasted until 1858. Bowlegs was one of the last Seminole leaders to surrender at the war's end. He and 123 of his followers relocated to Oklahoma.[11]

Osceola's mentor was the wise old war leader and medicine man Sam Jones (Abiaka). Abiaka continued to resist Seminole removal after Osceola's

Chief Billy Bowlegs

death. The Seminole were being hunted and pursued, and their resources were destroyed, but Abiaka refused to surrender. His steely determination and spirituality inspired his warriors to follow him. He never left the Florida Peninsula, and made his final camp in the Big Cypress Swamp.[12]

The Seminole Wars

First Seminole War, 1816–1818
—— Jackson's line of march
■ Military fort

Second Seminole War, 1835–1842
↳— Army column
✕ Battle site
■ Military fort

Third Seminole War, 1855–1858
■ Military fort
—— Seminole reservation boundary, 1827
------ Extent of reservation south of this line is uncertain since the legal description of 1823 was based on incomplete knowledge of the area.
▭ Seminole reservation, 1842
○ Indian town
1 Forts built during the Second Seminole War that were reactivated during the Third Seminole War.

The Seminole Wars of 1816 to 1858 covered most of the state of Florida.

Surviving in the Swamps

In 2016, Cultural Ambassador Everett Osceola described how the Seminole survived in the Florida swamps: "The U.S. government during the Seminole wars pushed us deep into the Florida Everglades. But we learned how to adapt to our environment and grew vegetation and fruit because the soil in the Everglades was very rich back then. The only meat for us to eat was garfish and alligators. We made use of every part of the alligator. The tail is where most of the meat is. We used the back of the alligator for armor and tied it around our shins and chest as a chest plate. The jawbone was used as a war club."

They also used what they learned in the Everglades to make a living: "Once the wars ended we slowly came out of the Everglades and traded with the stores. One of the biggest-selling items during the 1900s was alligator eggs, eaten as a delicacy and the shells used as decorations. The hides, too, sold. We'd catch the alligators, grab the eggs, and often let the gator go. Surprisingly, by the road some people saw Seminole men jumping into the water and grabbing alligators. They thought it was a show. They started giving us money, and soon we discovered we made more money doing this than trading."

"Alligator shows put food on the Seminole table for a good fifty years. . . . My family taught me to have profound respect for the alligator. They brought a lot of revenue and prosperity to the Seminole when we had nothing to eat."[13]

Seminole alligator demonstration

Chickees are shelters used for cooking, eating, and sleeping. The houses are constructed with palm leaves woven together for the roof and cypress logs posted into the ground. The Miccosukee continue to use chickees in the Everglades.

CHAPTER 4
LIFE AMONG THE SEMINOLES

In Oklahoma's Indian Territory, Native American cultures began to mix. Tribes from Mississippi brought their farming skills, which influenced the Seminole way of life. The Seminole planted corn (maize), beans, cane, millet, tobacco, and sunflowers. They also gathered nuts and wild fruit, hunted deer, and stored nut oil and bear fat. At this time, the Green Corn Ceremony, also called *puskita*, became an important Seminole tradition.[1]

The first Seminoles in northern Florida lived in log cabin–type homes, two stories high, with bedrooms upstairs.[2] This changed during the early 1800s when American soldiers tried to take Florida. Constantly pursued by U.S. troops, the Seminoles needed houses that could be built quickly and taken down just as fast. That is when they made the chickee. The chickee was a house on stilts. Cypress logs were posted in the ground, and palm leaves were woven together by vines or thin ropes. The floor was a wooden platform, and the roof was thatched. There were no walls—although in certain weather the family might hang sheets of canvas to keep warm and dry. The stilts protected the family from swamp animals and floods.

Inside the chickee, families slept on beds of hides. During the day, they rolled up their beds and hung them from the roof rafters. They also hung tools and cookware.

Chickees still exist throughout Florida. Building these open-air homes has become a booming business. However, most tribal homes in modern times are built with brick and stucco.

The dugout canoe was an important mode of transportation for many Native American groups, including the Seminole. It was used for hunting and trade in lakes, rivers, and swamps. The design and type of canoe each tribe used was based on the natural resources available. Leroy Osceola, a

Some Seminole dugout canoes were over 30 feet long. They could carry an entire family and all of their belongings.

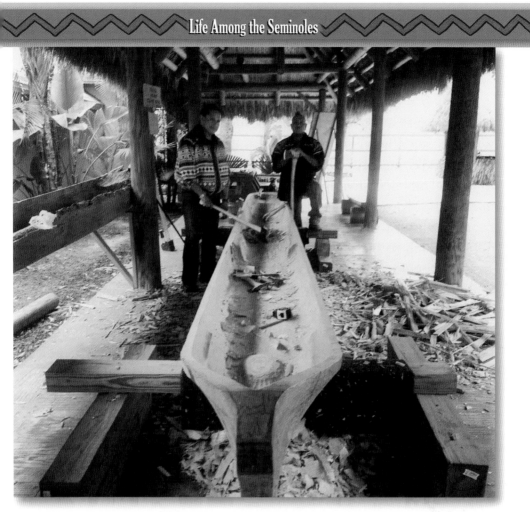

The canoes constructed by Leroy Osceola (right) are made in traditional designs from the eighteenth century. He hopes to keep the craft alive by teaching his sons how to build canoes.

full-blooded Miccosukee Seminole, is a canoe maker who lives in Florida. He makes 16-foot canoes from cypress wood. They are made in traditional designs from the 1700s.

According to him, the selection of the log is key. It has to be of the right length and diameter. The cypress tree is chopped down at the base. Once dried, the center is charred and then hollowed.

Osceola says the final touch is carving the push pole. It is used to propel and steer the canoe through the water. As one of the only canoe makers out there, Osceola fears this is becoming a lost art. He is teaching his sons how to build canoes, hoping they will pass it on and keep this craft alive.

Leroy Osceola describes Seminole society: "We are a matriarchal society, with eight clans. Each clan retains specific responsibilities and clan laws. All must abide by the overall tribal laws as well."

Seminole men and women dressed in patchwork clothing stitched with quilting. This decorative way of sewing brightly colored horizontal designs was developed by Seminole women. The technique has been passed from mothers to daughters for over sixty years.

According to Blackard and West, women also dressed in "floor-length skirts, gathered at the waist with an ornamented area and ruffle at knee length. The long sleeved blouse had an attached cape, trimmed with a

Seminole girls and women often wore brightly colored skirts and long, full dresses.

ruffle, halting at the shoulders. The women added glass necklace beads to enhance their outfits."[3]

During the 1800s, fashionable Seminole men wore loose shirts and turbans made with woolen shawls and decorated with silver and plumes. Some wore a beaded baldric sash and a belt that was leather, woven yarn, or beaded. In cold weather, Seminole men dressed in a colorful "long shirt" called the "medicine man's coat" with ruffles.

Photographs and drawings of Seminole men's hairstyles during the same time period show the sides of their heads shaved, with a fringe around their face. A lock of hair grew down from the crown of their head and ended in two braids. The women often wore long bangs, with the rest of their hair in a tight bun. It was rare to see a Seminole woman's hair down in public unless she was in mourning.

Many Seminoles continue to wear traditional hairstyles. As one article reveals, "In traditional

Seminole men often wore loose shirts and turbans made with woolen shawls and plumes. They dressed in a colorful "long shirt" with plenty of ruffles. The shirt was made to reach to the knees and had a split in the back for horseback riding.

33

Seminole Indian family in Musa Isle Indian Village - Miami, Florida.

families today, male babies have their hair ceremonially shaved at four months of age, leaving only a forelock. Their hair and nail clippings are carefully stored away. In the Seminole belief system . . . a person's hair had a strong use by supernaturals and in black magic, and in the old days it was carefully guarded."[4]

An Interview With Leroy Osceola: Tribal Councilman and Spokesman for the Sovereign Miccosukee Seminole Nation of Florida

Leroy Osceola

What was it like for you growing up?

Life was good because we were sheltered. In our culture, once you reach the age of 12 years old, you go to the next stage of learning and are considered an adult and ready for life. My parents' generation came out of the swamp and into the modern world. I grew up in the modern world, but we still had to work. We didn't go for handouts or anything. My father wrestled alligators and we did shows for tourists. If it was dry season we couldn't hunt, so we'd have to find work in the fields picking potatoes. When the waters returned we fished and hunted and lived off the land that way.

The local fish was garfish which was our delicacy; and mud fish, catfish, bream, and bass. Occasionally in the winter when the water is high, we'd catch snook in the fresh water. If we saw turtle, we would take them home to our camp and our parents would fix them up. Soft shell turtle, you boiled. The green turtle shell was roasted and the meat stewed. . . . .We still grow corn and wild pumpkin.

Today, the Seminole and other Native American tribes use aquaponic farming. Nutrient-rich water is pumped from a fish tank to plants in a greenhouse. The plants filter the water, cleaning it for the fish to use again. This farming method dates back to Aztec and early Asian cultures.

CHAPTER 5
SEMINOLE LIFE
TODAY

The Seminole tribes of Florida and Oklahoma are now federally recognized. This means the U.S. government respects their right to self-govern. The Seminole Nation of Oklahoma has the largest population (19,000) of Seminoles in the country. As the tribes began to exercise their sovereignty and purchase lands back, they have built new businesses in those areas.

One project is called aquaponics. This farming method combines aquaculture (fish farming) with hydroponics (growing plants in water). Aquaponics uses a system to grow fish and vegetables at the same time, using the same water. As Lewis Johnson, Assistant Chief Oklahoma Seminole Nation, explains, "It helps us grow protein and replenish foods for our diet."[1] Over the last 100 years, the Seminole diet has changed. Type 2 diabetes has become a major health issue. The key goal is to provide nutritious foods to regain overall health.

Johnson claims the Oklahoma Nation is the only tribe that has the original traditional form of Seminole government with an executive department, legislative branch, and judicial

Lewis Johnson

branch. "Our nation chose not to organize our constitution under the Oklahoma Indian Welfare Act or the Indian Reorganization Act," he says.

The Oklahoma Nation has been pressured to modernize, but Johnson strongly believes that won't happen. "That's our true identity—when we go back to our tribal community base and clans."

Everett Osceola reports that in the 1940s, the U.S. government needed to raise money for World War II. The country could not buy military equipment for World War II without cutting other budgets. They chose to cut the budget they had planned for the Seminoles. Part of the plan was to shut down the reservation. The Seminoles felt the government was not treating them as U.S. citizens. Tribal members demanded that Congress keep their promise and allow them 25 to 30 years to educate their youth. This demand was granted.

The logo for the Seminole Nation of Oklahoma, headquartered in Wewoka, Oklahoma. The Oklahoma group is the largest of the three federally recognized Seminole tribes.

The push for education in the Seminole community exceeded their expectations. "It took a lot of work, but within 50 years, we went from selling sandwiches and displaying arts and crafts on roadsides to running a billion-dollar industry."[2]

The Seminole Tribe of Florida has added new reservations, opened a new school, purchased the Hard Rock Café and Casinos, developed the Ah-Tah-Thi-Ki Museum and Kissimmee-Billie Swamp Safari, and expanded their stores and gaming enterprises.

Everett Osceola is thrilled with the tribe's prosperity, but he remembers a time when one of his two daughters came home from school after seeing a video. She said, "Dad, I don't want to be Indian anymore. We're bad people."

Shocked and disturbed, he discovered that many schools still showed videos of Indians portrayed as the bad guys and "savages." He made it his mission to teach the truth about Native Americans in the schools. He often brought a Seminole tribal member to classrooms for the students to meet. Today his daughters speak proudly of their ancestry.

"Seminoles have always been rich in family, culture, and language. If you let your culture go, then you cease to exist."

Seminole Stomp Dancers sometimes perform at public events.

An Interview with Everett Osceola:
Cultural Ambassador of the Seminole Tribe of Florida

Everett Osceola

What was life like for you growing up as a child?

I thought everyone lived the way I lived; working with cattle and horses and helping the family farm business. . . . I moved cows from one pasture to another and roped and marked the calves. I learned how to ride a horse, shoot a gun, and drive a stick shift pickup truck before I was ten.

My mother told me that outside people would never understand our ways. I went to summer school after participating in the Green Corn

Ceremony and had scratches on my arms, legs, back, and chest. My mother made me wear long-sleeve shirts and jackets even though it was hot. One of the Indian track stars took off his shirt to play basketball and the coach saw the scratches and marks on his body. He sent him and all us from the reservation to the principal's office. A representative from a child protection agency asked if we were being abused. The tribe had to go before the school board and explain this was part of our ceremony. . . . I realized my mother was right—outsiders don't understand who we are.

Many of my friends went to boarding school in Oklahoma, where there are many Indian schools. I stayed here in public school. I was the only native child in ninth and tenth grade. My hair was long and I got picked on and constantly bullied. The only person that came to my aid was a redneck who became a lifelong friend. I think our kinship formed because we had a lot in common. People in his town were also used to taking care of the cattle, fishing, protecting the land and keeping the Everglades clean, just like us.

I almost got into a fight with a guy from Nigeria the first time we met. He walked up and asked, "Why do you have long hair? I thought only girls have long hair." I wanted to fight until the counselor explained he barely spoke English and it was an innocent question. He just wanted to know if it was a part of my culture. Afterwards, we bonded and found that our cultures had many similarities, such as the bloodletting ceremony.

People are often surprised we celebrate Christmas and Thanksgiving, but it's really for family get-togethers. During these occasions, including birthdays, we cook deer meat, hog meat, pig meat, or hamburgers. Sometimes we slaughter a cow and cook it ourselves.

- There are eight Seminole clans: Panther, Bear, Deer, Wind, Bigtown, Bird, Snake, and Otter.

- Women are revered and respected. Children inherit the clan of the mother. If the last female in a clan passes on, the clan is considered extinct.

- A person could not marry within his or her clan, and arranged marriages were common. After the wedding, the groom moved to the home of the bride.

- The Upper Creek townspeople were called "Red Sticks." They used bundles of red sticks to measure time before the start of a war. If a bundle of 12 red sticks was delivered to an enemy, it meant they would be attacked in 12 days. Sometimes Creek warriors would leave a red war club at the scene of a battle.

- Many Seminoles now practice Christianity. However, they continue to practice their traditional religion as well, expressed through the Green Corn Ceremony.

- On December 14, 1979, the Seminoles became the first Native American tribe to open a casino on Indian lands. Other tribes soon followed in what proved to be a profitable industry.

- Black Seminoles now live throughout the United States, but they are mostly in Oklahoma, Texas, and Florida. Some have moved to Mexico and the Bahamas.

- Seminole Chief Billy Bowlegs often wore a silver headband with ostrich feathers and bandoliers of braided wool and beadwork.

- Osceola's wife was Che-cho-ter, or Morning Dew. Historians describe her as possibly of African descent and remarkably beautiful.

- Before the wars, Osceola and a West Point graduate named John Graham became friends. The two men exchanged gifts and taught each other their languages. During the battle of Withlacoochee, Osceola cautioned his warriors not to fire on Lieutenant Graham, and it saved his life.

1540	The Spanish arrive in Florida.
1804	Osceola is born as William Powell.
1817	In the First Seminole War, U.S. soldiers invade Spanish Florida. They burn Seminole towns and capture fugitve slaves.
1819	Florida becomes a U.S. territory.
1821	Andrew Jackson is appointed governor of Florida. Spain sells Florida to the United States for $5 million.
1823	Seminoles and U.S. government agents sign a treaty of "peace and friendship" at Moultrie Creek in Florida.
1830	U.S. President Andrew Jackson signs the Indian Removal Act.
1835	The Second Seminole War begins in Florida.
1838	Osceola dies in prison.
1842	The Second Seminole War ends; 3,800 Seminole people are relocated to Indian Territory.
1855	The Third Seminole War begins in Florida. Three years later, Chief Billy Bowlegs is one of the last Seminole leaders to surrender.
1890	Seminoles and settlers begin to trade peacefully on the Florida Everglades border.
1900	Seminoles begin to make patchwork designs.
1920s	South Florida tourism booms. Seminoles sell crafts and wrestle alligators.
1928	The Tamiami Trail opens. It is the first road across the Everglades from Tampa to Miami.
1957	The Seminole Tribe of Florida is recognized by the federal government.
1962	The Miccosukee Seminole tribe of Florida receives recognition from the U.S. government. It drafts a constitution and forms a tribal government. Eventually the tribe gains reservation lands along the Tamiami Trail.
1974	Congress passes the Indian Self-Determination and Education Assistance Act, which gives the tribe greater control over its political and economic affairs.
1979	Seminole Casino Hollywood opens in Hollywood, Florida.
1995	Native Americans have been in Florida for over 12,000 years.
2010	The State of Florida and Seminole Tribe of Florida agree on the Seminole Gaming Compact. It gives the tribe a monopoly over certain types of gaming in exchange for a portion of the casino profits.
2016	The Seminole Tribe of Florida buys the Hard Rock Hotel and Casino brand, called Hard Rock International. They now own all Hard Rock businesses around the world.

Chapter One: The Ceremony

1. Edward J. Rielly, *Legends of American Resistance* (Santa Barbara: Greenwood, 2011), p. 93.
2. Ojibwa, "The Green Corn Ceremony," May 5, 2011, http://nativeamericannetroots.net/diary/951
3. Thom Hatch, *Osceola and the Great Seminole War: A Struggle for Justice and Freedom* (New York: St. Martin's Press, 2012), p. 43.
4. Willie Johns, "Circle of Dance: Seminole Stomp Dance," *Smithsonian National Museum of the American Indian* 2011, http://nmai.si.edu/static/exhibitions/circleofdance/seminole.html#essay
5. Hatch, p. 43.

Chapter Two: The Beginnings

1. Jerry Wilkinson, "Historic Florida Indians" http://www.keyshistory.org/histindians.html
2. Dru J. Murray, "The Unconquered Seminoles, *Florida History Native Peoples*," http://www.abfla.com/1tocf/seminole/semhistory.html
3. Thom Hatch, *Osceola and the Great Seminole War: A Struggle for Justice and Freedom* (New York: St. Martin's Press, 2012), p. 30.
4. Murray.
5. Hatch, pp. 31–32

Chapter Three: The Invaders, War, and Relocation

1. Thom Hatch, *Osceola and the Great Seminole War: A Struggle for Justice and Freedom* (New York: St. Martin's Press, 2012), p. 31.
2. Dru J. Murray, "The Unconquered Seminoles, *Florida History Native Peoples*, "http://www.abfla.com/1tocf/seminole/semhistory.html
3. Anton Treuer, *Atlas of Indian Nations* (Washington, D.C.: National Geographic, 2014), p. 76.
4. Hatch, pp. 55–56.

5. Murray.
6. Florida Department of State, "The Seminole Wars," http://dos.myflorida.com/florida-facts/florida-history/seminole-history/the-seminole-wars/
7. Murray.
8. Florida Department of State, "The Seminole Wars."/
9. Edward J. Rielly, *Legends of American Resistance* (Santa Barbara: Greenwood, 2011), pp. 104–105.
10. Interview with Leroy Johnson, Assistant Chief, Oklahoma Seminole Nation.
11. Treuer, p. 69.
12. Seminole Tribe of Florida, "Osceola and Abiaka," http://www.semtribe.com/History/OsceolaandAbiaka.aspx
13. Interview with Cultural Ambassador Everett Osceola.

Chapter Four: Seminole Life

1. Michael G. Johnson, *Native Tribes of North America* (Buffalo: Firefly Books, 2014), p. 78.
2. Ernie Tiger, "Chickees Provided Early Housing," Seminole Tribe of Florida, http://www.semtribe.com/Culture/Chickee.aspx
3. David M. Blackyard and Patsy West, "Seminole Clothing, Seminole Tribe of Florida," http://www.semtribe.com/Culture/SeminoleClothing.aspx
4. Patsy West, "Hairstyle—Reflections #136," Seminole Tribe of Florida, http://www.semtribe.com/Culture/Hairstyle.aspx

Chapter Five: Seminole Life Today

1. Interview with Assistant Chief Lewis Johnson, Oklahoma Seminole Nation.
2. Interview with Cultural Ambassador Everett Osceola, Seminole Tribe of Florida.

Books

Annino, J.G. *She Sang Promise: The Story of Betty Mae Jumper, Seminole Tribal Leader*. Washington, D.C.: National Geographic Children's Books, 2010.

Charles Rivers Editors. *Native American Tribes: The History and Culture of the Seminole*. Create Space Independent Publishing Platform, 2003.

Field, Ron. *The Seminole Wars 1818–58* (Men-at-Arms). Oxford: Osprey Publishing, 2009.

George, Gale. *Seminole (Spotlight on Native Americans)*. New York: PowerKids Press, 2016.

Johnson, Michael G. *Native Tribes of North America*. Buffalo: Firefly Books, 2014.

Sandford, William R. *Seminole Chief Osceola (Native American Chiefs and Warriors)*. Berkeley Heights, NJ: Enslow Publishers, 2013.

Works Consulted

This book is based on the author's personal interviews with the following people:

Lewis Johnson, Assistant Chief Oklahoma Seminole Nation, July 22, 2016

Everett Osceola, Cultural Ambassador, July 21, 2016

Leroy Osceola, Councilman & Spokesperson, July 20, 2016

and on the following sources:

Edwards, Owen. "A Seminole Warrior Cloaked in Defiance." *Smithsonian Magazine*, October 2010. http://www.smithsonianmag.com/history/a-seminole-warrior-cloaked-in-defiance-60004300/?no-ist

Florida Center for Instructional Technology. *Exploring Florida*. "The Seminole Wars." College of Education, University of South Florida, 2002. http://fcit.usf.edu/florida/lessons/sem_war/sem_war1.htm

Hatch, Thom. *Osceola and the Great Seminole War: A Struggle for Justice and Freedom*. New York: St. Martin's Press, 2012.

Johns, Willie. "Circle of Dance: Seminole Stomp Dance." *Smithsonian National Museum of the American Indian*, 2011. http://nmai.si.edu/static/exhibitions/circleofdance/seminole.html#essay

Monticello.org: "President Jefferson and the Indian Nations," https://www.monticello.org/site/jefferson/president-jefferson-and-indian-nations

Pleasants, Julian M. *Seminole Voices: Reflections on Their Changing Society, 1970–2000* (Indians of the Southeast). Lincoln: University of Nebraska Press, 2010.

Rielly, Edward J. *Legends of American Resistance*. Santa Barbara: Greenwood, 2011.

The Seminole Tribe of Florida. http://www.semtribe.com

Treuer, Anton. *Atlas of Indian Nations*. Washington, D.C.: National Geographic, 2014.

Wilkinson, Jerry. "Historic Florida Indians." Historical Preservation Society of the Upper Keys. http://www.keyshistory.org/histindians.html

Wittich, Katarina. "Black Seminoles: A Historical Overview." http://lestweforget.hamptonu.edu/page.cfm?uuid=9FEC2EBF-C16B-DB1C-B42C1586C7F4610F

Internet Reading

Ducksters: Native Americans, "Seminole Tribe." http://www.ducksters.com/history/native_americans/seminole_tribe.php

Florida Department of State: "Seminole History." http://dos.myflorida.com/florida-facts/florida-history/seminole-history/

Native Heritage Project: Seminole Chief Osceola, Billy Powell https://nativeheritageproject.com/2014/05/10/seminole-chief-osceola-billy-powell/

apprentice (uh-PREN-tiss)—A student learning the trade of a master.

aquaponics (ak-wah-PAH-niks)—A system of farming that uses water: waste from fish fertilizes plants, which then purify the water for the fish.

bandolier (ban-doh-LEER)—A belt worn over the shoulder and across the chest, usually used to carry a weapon or to hold bullets.

casino (kuh-SEE-noh)—A business that features gambling.

confederacy (kun-FED-er-ruh-see)—A group of people joined together for a cause.

guerrilla (guh-RIL-uh) **warfare**—Warfare involving hit-and-run tactics, ambushes, and other stealthy forms of attack.

Indian Reservation (reh-zer-VAY-shun)—A legally assigned area of land set aside for Native Americans.

militia (mil-IH-shuh)—A group of non-soldiers who are trained to fight as an army in case of emergency.

rite (RYT)—An act that is part of a religious ceremony.

ritual (RIT-choo-ul)—A formal ceremony that is always done in the same way.

shackle (SHAK-ul)—To bind a person's hands and ankles using cuffs connected by a chain.

sovereign (SOV-er-in)—Self-governing.

supernaturals (soo-per-NACH-er-uhls)—People who have or seem to have magical powers.

symbolize (SIM-boh-lyz)—To stand for an idea; for example, in Seminole culture, the eagle symbolizes bravery.

trek (TREK)—To walk on a long journey.

MEET THE
AUTHOR

Wayne L. Wilson is a novelist and screenwriter, and he has written numerous biographical and historical books for children and young adults. He wrote the acclaimed children's book *Kate the Ghost Dog: Coping With the Death of a Pet*. He received his Master of Arts in Education from UCLA, and continues to live in California.